LUVTLK!

ltle bk
of luv
txt

WAN2HELP?

We are constantly updating our files of text messages and emoticons for the next edition of **LUVTLK!** and our other text message books. If you would like to add variations of your own please e-mail us at **jokes@michaelomarabooks.com**

We will let you know if your additions are going to be included. Thank you

LUVTLK!

ltle bk

of luv

txt

evil-i

First published in Great Britain in 2001 by
Michael O'Mara Books Limited
9 Lion Yard
Tremadoc Road
London SW4 7NQ

A CIP catalogue record for this book is available from the British Library

ISBN 1-85479-890-1

1 3 5 7 9 10 8 6 4 2

Devised and compiled by Gabrielle Mander

Cover Design: Design 23
Telephone supplied and used by kind permission of Motorola.

Designed and typeset by Design 23

www.mombooks.com

Made and printed in Great Britain by William Clowes, Beccles, Suffolk

CONTENTS

SndW/AGrn
  Send with a grin   6

Pur&Smple?
  The acme of love acronyms for the
  pure at heart   8

Wa$aNcGLkeUDoinInAPlcLkeThs
  Making friends and influencing people   22

10SecLuv?
  Fast-track emoticons   32

LuvLines!
  Words of love for smooth operators   44

SoPyStuF!
  From the bard to the Bible – love poems   66

Bak2YaROts
  Basic acronyms and abbreviations   79

MdgtMsges
  Even shorter shorthand for fast talkers   93

SndW/AGrn

Send with a grin

All mobile phones vary, but access to the messaging service is usually simple.Go to '**Menu**' and scroll to '**Messages**' then to '**Message Editor**'. Compose your message by using the letter and number keys on your phone. Each key represents more than one letter and symbol in both upper and lower case so you need to press repeatedly until the letter you want appears. Press the # key to stop the letter flashing. When your message is complete press 'ok' and your message will be sent. 'Message-speak' is self-explanatory, but a few hints might be useful. The fewer characters that you use without spaces between words, the speedier and less expensive your message will be both to send and receive. Start each new word with a capital letter. When a capital appears at the end of a word it means a long vowel sound. When it appears in the middle it means a double letter: so **BaB = Baby** and **BuBle = Bubble**. A $ sign means double **S** thus **SC$ = Success** and a capital **T = The**. A full list of basic shortcuts and clever abbreviations are given in **Bak2YaROts** and special tricks appear in each chapter! Fast and fun, your love life will change forever with **LUVTLK!**

Pur&Smple?

The acme of love acronyms for the pure at heart

AML	all my love
BBSD	be back soon darling
BEG	big evil grin
BF	boy friend
BGWM	be gentle with me (please)
BURMA	be upstairs ready my angel

CSG	chuckle, snicker, grin
CSThnknAU	can't stop thinking about you
CUIMD	see you in my dreams
CUL8R	see you later
CW2CU	can't wait to see you
CW2HU	can't wait to hold you
DLTBBB	don't let the bed bugs bite
ETUSGICAL	every time you say goodbye I cry a little

4EVRYRS	forever yours
FEITNEdIM	feel the need in me
FOBL	fell outta bed laughing
FYEO	for your eyes only
GF	girl friend
GGFN	gotta go for now
GMTA	great minds think alike
GOA	glad all over

GOdLuvinAEz2Fnd
good loving ain't
easy to find

GrOvyBaB groovy baby

GrwOldWivMe?
grow old with me?

GSOH good salary, own home

GTSY glad to see you

HAGN have a good night

HDEpIYLuv? how deep is your love?

HITULThtILuvU?   have I told you lately that I love you?

HLuvWT   have love will travel

HMTMXM   hold me, thrill me, kiss me

HOHIL   head over heels in love

Hot4U   hot for you

HotLuv   hot love

HotX3   (feeling) hot, hot, hot

H&K   hug and kiss

HWI4U?   how was it for you?

IC**WenUXMe

I see stars when you kiss me

ICLW\YLuv   I can't live without your love

IHTFP   I have truly found paradise

IJC2SalLuvU

I just called to say I love you

ILUVU   I love you

ILUVUMED   I love you more each day

IMBLuv   it must be love

13

IMYaDstny   I am your destiny

IOHiis4U   I only have eyes for you

IOWAN2BWU
        I only want to be with you

I WANU   I want you

I WLAlwys LuvU
        I will always love you

JTLUNoILuvU
    just to let you know
    I love you

JTM   Je t'aime

KIT   keep in touch

KOTC   kiss on the cheek

KOTL   kiss on the lips

LLL   lay lady lay

LTNC   long time no see

LuvMnsNvrHvin2
SaYaSRy   love means never having
to say you're sorry

LuvYa   love you

LUWAM<3   love you with all my heart

MBURBMJ   my but you're beautiful
Miss Jones

MkeMyDaSa+!
    make my day, say yes

NE1WHdA<3Wld
NoTht ILuvU
    anyone who had a heart…
would know that I love you

OBTWIAU	oh, by the way I adore you
OIC	oh I see
OL	old lady (girlfriend, wife)
OM	old man (boyfriend, husband)
PM	private message
QT	cutie
ROFWivU	rolling on the floor with you
RSN	really soon now

Salt&ILDoIt	say it and I'll do it
SETE	smiling ear to ear
SO	significant other
SRy	sorry
SRySEms2B THrdst Wrd	sorry seems to be the hardest word
SWALK	sent with a loving kiss
TDTU	totally devoted to you
THNQ	thank you

TMIY   take me I'm yours

TOY   thinking of you

U2MeREvrythng
      you to me are everything

VVCAMCS?   voulez-vous couchez avec
      moi ce soir?

WICIWIW   what I see is what I want

WLUMRyMe?
      will you marry me?

WLUStLLuvMe2moro?
      will you still love me
      tomorrow?

WUSIWUG	what you see is what you get
+! +! +!	YES! YES! YES!
- ! - ! - !	NO! NO! NO!
X	kiss
XMeQk	kiss me quick
Xoxoxoxo	hugs and kisses
XclusvlyYas	exclusively yours
YBS	you'll be sorry
YG	young gentleman

YL	young lady
* H *	hug
* X *	kiss
* W *	wink

Wa$aNcGLkeUDoi nInAPlcLkeThs?

Making friends and influencing people

ALThosCrvs&MeWivNoBrks
> all those curves and me
> with no brakes

CnIFlrtWivU?
> can I flirt with you?

DdUHrtYasIfWenUFeLFrmHvn?
> did you hurt yourself when
> you fell from heaven?

DntUNoMeFrmSumwer?

  don't you know me from
  somewhere?

DoUMndIfIFntsizAbtU?

  do you mind if I fantasize
  about you?

DoUWan2ShgOrShldISaSRy?

  do you want to shag or
  should I apologize?

DtWeGo2DFrtSchls?

  didn't we go to different
  schools?

DrpM drop 'em

GetYaCotUvePuLd
> get your coat you've
> pulled

HaBaBWan2GtLcky?
> hey baby, want to get
> lucky?

HrsYaChnc2Gt2NoMe
> here's your chance to get
> to know me

HwAbtU&IGtOutOfThseWetClthes?
> how about you and I get
> out of these wet clothes?

**(After licking finger and touching
yourself and her/him on shoulder)**

HwDoULkMeSoFa?

how do you like me so far?

IdLOkGOdOnU

I'd look good on you

IfHeDsntShwUpImRtHre

if he doesn't show up,
I'm right here

**IflSedUHdAButiful
BdyWldUHldItAgnstMe?**

if I said you had a beautiful
body would you hold it
against me?

ImA*vinRtst&IWan2EatU

I'm a starving artist and
I want to eat you

IMi$MyTDyBerWldUSlEpWivMe?

I miss my teddy bear.
Would you sleep with me?

ImLOkn4AFrndDoUWan2BMyFrnd?

I'm looking for a friend.
Do you want to be my
friend?

InMyABCIWldPutU&ITgthr

in my alphabet I would put
you and I together

IvBinWtchnUNotWtchnMe

> I've been watching you
> not watching me

IWldDiHPyIfISawUNkdJst1nc

> I would die happy if I saw
> you naked just once

MaIEndThsSntncWivAPropstn?
>may I end this sentence
>with a proposition?

NceDr$CnITlkUOutOfIt?
>nice dress, can I talk
>you out of it?

PctrThsUMeBblesx2
>Picture this – you, me,
>bubble baths and
>champagne

RURdy2GoHmeNw?
>are you ready to go
>home now?

RUUP4IT?   are you up for it?

ShLICaLUOrNdgU4Bfst2moro?

>shall I call you or nudge
>you for breakfast
>tomorrow?

SoHwAmIDoin?

>so...how am I doing?

SOSImLstWchWa2yaPlce?

>help, I'm lost – which way
>to your place?

SRy2StareIWan2RmbrYaFce4MyDrms

>excuse me, do you mind if
>I stare at you for a minute?
>I want to remember your
>face for my dreams

ThtDr$WldLOkGrtOnMyBdrOmFlr

that dress would look great
on my bedroom floor

TkeAChnceOnMe?

        take a chance on me?

WldULkeSum12MxWivYaDrnk?

        would you like someone
        to mix with your drink?

WotCnIDo2MkeUBMne?

        what can I do to make you
        be mine?

XcusMeCnUGivMeDrctns2Ya<3?

        excuse me, can you
        give me directions to
        your heart?

1OSecLuV?

Fast-track emoticons

:-	male
➤	female
O:-)	angel
0*-)	angel winking
➤-::-D	I am smitten by Cupid's arrow
&;-P	I am a suave guy on the make

;->	devilish wink
*:-} 8 O	I am a cool chick on the make
(o)(o)	I am a well-endowed female
^	all clear for tonight
P-)	yes, I am coming on to you
~:-P	I am thinking and steaming
(o_o)	I am shocked
@*&$!%	you know what that means

:-*;	I am blowing you a kiss
:-9	I am licking my lips
**-(	I am very, very shocked
:-)~	I am drooling (in anticipation)
*;~I	I am a lady replying by closing both eyes and puffing nonchalantly on her cigarette
:-e	of course I'm disappointed, I can't wait to see you

`<X`	I am crazy about you and sending you a wet kiss
`*^_^*`	you are making me blush (Japanese style)
`*^o^*`	this is so exciting
`+<#^v`	I am your knight in shining armour (profile)
`:-P`	my tongue is hanging out in anticipation and I want to lick your neck
`;-S`	I kind of like it

:()	I could talk to you all night
o:-)	you are my angel
:~)	I feel drunk with love
:-6	I am losing sleep over you
:-9	you are delicious, yummy
:->	you look devilishly good
:-I	I need to know if you love me
:*)	I can't believe that you are serious

:~/	I'm a bit mixed up just now
:-\	I can't make up my mind about you
:-O	I am surprised you didn't guess how I feel
:->	of course you make me happy
(:-\	I am VERY sad that we can't be together
(@ @)	you must be joking – of course I miss you!

:-{}	a hot and heavy kiss awaits you
@}>'-,—	a rose for you
12x—<—@	a dozen roses for you
8-)	of course there is no other man/woman
:@	it's true, I swear
>	it's female intuition
(:-...	I am heart-broken

:-S	I am confused
:*(	I am crying softly
:-C	I am really missing you
>:-<	I'm mad for you
I-I	this is me asleep
:-[	pouting works in the movies
:'-)	I am so happy, I am crying
:-{}	I am wearing lipstick

((H)))	a big hug
(:-*	kissing
:*	kisses
I*	kiss (eyes closed)
:-X	a big wet kiss
:-) (-: + :-o o-: + :-Pd-:	
	kissing (sequence)
:-I	hmmm
:-0	ohhhhhh!
I:-O	big ohhhhhh!

8-]	'wow, maaan'
8O	omigod!
***I**	oh, what a beautiful sunset!
I[*]	my heart is exploding with happiness NOW!!!!!
,:	I am rendered powerless by my love
:)	smile
=)	smile
=o)	smile

=O)	smile
:o)	smile
:O)	smile
(*_*)	I am in love
:~(~~~	I am moved to tears
<3	I love you
(-_-)	this is my secret smile (sideways)
:-X	many kisses
;-)=)	I can't stop grinning

I-() I-()	two sleepy people by dawn's early light, too much in love to say good night
#-)	we really have to get some sleep – I can't go on partying all night, every night
((((name))))	hug
(()):**	hugs and kisses

LuvLines!

Words of love for smooth operators

ADctd2Luv addicted to love

Adrd&Xplrd adored and explored

AintNoMntnHiEnuf2KEpMeFrmU
ain't no mountain high
enough to keep me
from you

Aint0LkeTRThngBaB
ain't nothing like the real
thing baby

ALlHav2DoIsDrm
        all I have to do is dream

ALIWanIsU   all I want is you

ALNiteLng   all night long

ALOr0   all or nothing

ALtleLuv?   a little love?

Alwys&4ever
        always and forever

&ILuvUSo   and I love you so

0:-) iis   angel eyes

BaBItsU   baby it's you

BdBy   bad boy

BFrEWivYa<3

    be free with your heart

Brn2BMyBaB

    born to be my baby

CldItBMgic?

    could it be magic?

Cld9?   cloud 9?

CntGtEnufOfU

    can't get enough of you

CntHlpFLinInLuvWivU
> can't help falling in love
> with you

CU2Nite@8YrPlce?
> see you tonight at 8 at your
> place?

Cum2gthrRiteNow
> come together right now

< :-) or 0: -) ?
> devil or angel?

DdntIBloYaMndThsTime?
> didn't I blow your mind
> this time?

DoNeThngUWan2Do
> do anything you want to do

DoWotUDo2Me
> do what you do to me

DrwninInTCOLuv
> drowning in the sea of love

Ndl$Luv endless love

EvrlstnLuv everlasting love

EvryLtleThngUDoIsMgic
every little thing you
do is magic

EvryMveUMkeILBWtchnU
every move you make I'll
be watching you

4evrInLuv forever in love

4evrKndOfLuv
forever kind of love

GMeSumLuvin
      gimme some lovin'

GMeMeYaLuvin
      give me your loving

GnaMakUAnOFrUCntRfs
      gonna make you an offer
      you can't refuse

GoTaBASn   gotta be a sin

GotTTme?   got the time?

GtOnUpGtOnDwn
      get on up, get on down

GtOutaMyDrms&In2MyLfe
get out of my dreams and
into my life

HavITRite?   have I the right?

HldMeClse   hold me close

HlpMeMkeItThruTNite
help me make it through
the night

HowWasIt4U?
how was it for you?

HplSlyInLuvWivU
hopelessly in love with you

IBlveInMrclsUSxyThng

I believe in miracles, you sexy thing

ICnLuvULkeTht

I can love you like that

IDntDsrveU – U 0 :-)

I don't deserve you – you angel

IfAPcturPntsKWrds
ThnYCntIPnt U?

if a picture paints a thousand words then why can't I paint you?

IFU   I feel you

IfUCntBWivT1
ULuvLuvT1YaWiv

>if you can't be with the one
>you love, love the one
>you're with.

IfUGoT2GoGoNow
OrElseUGot2StaALNite

>if you gotta go go now
>or else you've got to stay
>all night

IGotUBbe   I got you babe

ILBTher4U   I'll be there for you

ILKEpYaDrmsAliv

               I'll keep your dreams alive

ILTUWotIWanWotIRLyRLyWan

               I'll tell you what I want,
               what I really, really want

ILuvUMorThnWrdsCnsa

               I love you more than
               words can say

ImInIt4Luv   I'm in it for love

ImRdy4Luv   I'm ready for love

ImT14U   I'm the one for you

INEdU2Nite   I need you tonight

ItMstBLuv   It must be love

ItsNowOrNvr
it's now or never

IWan2WakUEvryDaWivU
I want to wake up every
day with you

JstCLMe   just call me

JstP$nThru just passing through

LIL let it last

LolLuvUWntUTLMeYaNme?
hello, I love you won't you
tell me your name?

LstInU lost in you

LtsGt2gthr   let's get together

LtsIntr:-) BaB
        let's interface baby

LtsMakThsANite2Rmba
        let's make this a night to
        remember

LuvIsTDrug   love is the drug

LuvMeLuvMyDog
        love me, love my dog

LuvMeWrm&Tndr
        love me warm and tender

LuvOr0 love or nothing

Luv2LuvUBaB
love to love you baby

LuvWLKEpUs2gthr
love will keep us together

M$ULkeCraZ miss you like crazy

No1CnEvrTkeYaPlce
no-one can ever take
your place

NvrNuALuvLkeThsB4
never knew a love like
this before

1<3BtwEn2   one heart between two

OnlyU   only you

OWotAFElin   oh what a feeling

OWntUStaJstALtleBitLngr?
   oh, won't you stay just a
   little bit longer?

PlsDntGo   please don't go

PmpUpTVolum
   pump up the volume

PrTyLtle 0:-)iis
   pretty little angel eyes

RckMeBaB rock me baby

RdMyLps-ILUVU
　　　　　　read my lips - I love you

RMB ring my bell

RmbaYaMne
　　　　　　remember you're mine

ResQMe rescue me

Slav2Luv slave to love

SoInLuvWivU
　　　　　　so in love with you

StaWivMeBaB
       stay with me baby

StckOnU   stuck on you

StndByYaMan
       stand by your man

SvnALMyLuv4U
       saving all my love for you

2gthrWeRButiful
       together we are beautiful

2Hot2Hndle   too hot to handle

TGILuvWivU

    this guy's/girl's in love
    with you

TkeMyHndTkeMyHleLfe2
CosICntSOS
FLinInLuvWivU

    take my hand, take my
    whole life too
    'cos I can't help falling in
    love with you

TLMeImDrmn

    tell me I'm dreaming

TonlyThngThtLOksGOdOnMeIsU

    the only thing that looks
    good on me is you

TruLuv   true love

UBlwMyMnd

       you blow my mind

UCnDoMgic   you can do magic

UDoIt4Me   you do it for me

U+Me=Luv   you + me = love

UDntHav2SaULuvMe

       you don't have to say you
       love me

UdoSumthn2Me

       you do something to me

ULiteMyFre you light my fire

UM UM UM UM UM UM
um um um um um um

URT1 you are the one

URTBstThngThtsEvrHPnd2Me
you're the best thing that's
ever happened to me

U2MeREvryThng
you to me are everything

WenCnICUAgn?
when can I see you again?

WenEvrULOkUpTherShLIB
>whenever you look up
>there shall I be

Wshn&Hpn&Thnkn&Prayn
>wishing and hoping and
>thinking and praying

Wt4MeDrlin   wait for me darling

WUWH   wish you were here

ZngWntTStrngsOfMy<3
>zing went the strings of my
>heart

SoPyStuF!

From the bard to the Bible – love poems

**Wen IM Nr U Drst
I Dre Nt Spk Ya Nme**

When I am near you, dearest
I dare not speak your name.

**Bsde T 1 I Luv I Lie
Hnd On Hnd Si On Si**

Beside the one I love I lie
Hand on hand, sigh on sigh.

Mi Luv Is TL As Ne Mntn
Hi As T Hiest Tree

My love is tall as any mountain
High as the highest tree.

I Luv U Da By Da & Yr By Yr
Mre & Mre Tr By Tr

I love you day by day and year by year
more and more, tear by tear.

AL Thghts AL P$ons
AL Dlits
Wotevr Strs Ths Mrtl Frm
AL R But Mnsters Of Luv
& FEd His Scrd Flme

All thoughts, all passions,
All delights,
Whatever stirs this mortal frame,
All are but ministers of Love.
And feed his sacred flame.

Samuel Taylor Coleridge

**U R Alwys Nu
T Lst Of Ya XXX
Ws Evr T SwEtst**

You are always new.
The last of your kisses
Was ever the sweetest…

John Keats

E>

We Wer 2 & Hd Bt 1 <3

We were two and had but one heart.

François Villon

Dbt thou T *** R Fre
Dbt Tht T Sun Doth Mve
Dbt Trth 2 B a Liar
Bt Nvr Dbt I Luv

Doubt thou the stars are fire;
Doubt that the sun doth move;
Doubt truth to be a liar;
But never doubt I love.

William Shakespeare

O My Luvs Lke a Rd Rd Rse
Thts Nwly Sprng in Jne
O My Luvs Lke T Mlode
Thts SwEtly Plyed in Tne

O, my love's like a red red rose
That's newly sprung in June;
O, my love's like the melodie
That's sweetly play'd in tune.

Robert Burns

Whoso Luvs Blves
T ImpSble

Whoso loves believes
the impossible.

2 Hmn Luvs Mke 1 Dvne

Two human loves make one divine.

Elizabeth Barrett Browning

Luv LOks Nt Wiv T iis
Bt Wiv T Mnd

Love looks not with the eyes
But with the mind.

William Shakespeare

AL Luv is SwEt
Gvn or Rtrnd
CMon as Lite is Luv
& its Fmlr Voice Wearies
Nt Evr

All love is sweet
Given or returned.
Common as light is love;
And its familiar voice wearies not ever.

Percy Bysshe Shelley

Lt Him X Me Wiv T XXs
Of His Mouth 4 Thy Luv
Is BTr Thn Win

Let him kiss me with the kisses
Of his mouth: for thy love
Is better than wine.

Song of Solomon 1:2

Giv Me K XXs Thn
A Hndrd, Thn K Mor

Give me a thousand kisses, then
A hundred, then a thousand more.

Catullus

A Thng of ButE is a Jy 4evr
Its LuvlinS IncrEs it WL Nvr
PS into 0thineS

A thing of beauty is a joy forever:
Its loveliness increases; it will never
Pass into nothingness.

John Keats

Only R Luv Hth No DcA
Ths No 2moro Hath
Nor Ystrda
RNin It Nvr Rns
Frm Us Awy
Bt Trly KEps Hs 1st Lst
Evrlstin Da

Only our love hath no decay;
This, no tomorrow hath,
Nor yesterday,
Running it never runs
From us away,
But truly keeps his first, last
Everlasting day

John Donne

Bak2YaR0ts

Basic acronyms and abbreviations

AAM   as a matter of fact

AB   ah bless!

AFAIC   as far as I'm concerned

AFAIK   as far as I know

AKA   also known as

ASAP   as soon as possible

ATB	all the best
B	be
BBFN	bye bye for now
BCNU	be seeing you
B4	before
BFN	bye for now
BRB	be right back
BTW	by the way
Bwd	backward

BYKT	but you knew that
C	see
CMIIW	correct me if I'm wrong
CU	see you
CYA	see you
Doin	doing
EOL	end of lecture
FAQ	frequently asked question(s)
FITB	fill in the blank

F2T	free to talk
Fwd	forward
FWIW	for what it's worth
FYI	for your information
GG	good game
Gonna	going to
Gr8	great
HAND	have a nice day
H8	hate

HTH	hope this/to help(s)
IAC	in any case
IAE	in any event
ICL	in Christian love
IDK	I don't know
IIRC	if I recall correctly
IMCO	in my considered opinion
IMHO	in my humble opinion
IMNSHO	in my not so humble opinion

IMO	in my opinion
IOW	in other words
ITYFIR	I think you'll find I'm right
IYDKIDKWD	if you don't know I don't know who does
IYKWIM	If you know what I mean
IYKWIMAITYD	if you know what I mean and I think you do
IYSS	if you say so
JM2p	just my 2 penny-worth

L8	late
L8r	later
Luv	love
LOL	lots of luck or laughing out loud
MGB	may God bless
MHOTY	my hat's off to you
MMDP	make my day punk!
Mob	mobile
Msg	message

MYOB	mind your own business
NE	any
NE1	anyone
NH	nice hand
NO1	no one
NRN	no reply necessary
OIC	oh, I see
OTOH	on the other hand
PCM	please call me

PLS	please
PPL	people
PS	post script
R	are
ROF	rolling on the floor
ROTFL	rolling on the floor laughing
RU?	are you?
RUOK?	are you OK?
SIT	stay in touch

SITD	still in the dark
SMS	short message service
SOHF	sense of humour failure
SOME1	someone
Stra	stray
SWG	scientific wild guess
THNQ	thank you
Thx	thanks
TIA	thanks in advance

TIC	tongue in cheek
Ti2GO	time to go
TPTB	the powers that be
TTFN	ta ta for now
TTUL	talk to you later
TWIMC	to whom it may concern
TUVM	thank you very much
U	you
UR	you are

WAN2	want to
WAN2TLK?	want to talk?
W/	with
Wknd	weekend
WRT	with respect to
WTTW	word to the wise
YKWYCD	you know what you can do
YMMV	your mileage may vary (you may not have the same luck I did)

YA	your
YTLKIN2ME?	
	you talking to me?
YWIA	you're welcome in advance
YYSSW	yeah, yeah, sure, sure, whatever
1dafL	wonderful
2	to, too
2day	today
2moro	tomorrow

2nite	tonight
3sum	threesome
4	for
<G>	grinning
<J>	joking
<L>	laughing
<O>	shouting
<S>	smiling
<Y>	yawning

Mdgtmsges

Even shorter shorthand for really fast talkers

:)	happy
:]	friendly
=)	friendly
:}	what?
:D	laughter
:) :) :)	loud guffaw

:I	hmmm...
;)	smirking
:(	sad
; (	chin up
:O	yelling.

The Little Book of Irish Grannies' Remedies -
    ISBN 1-85479-828-6
The Little Book of Scottish Grannies' Remedies -
    ISBN 1-85479-829-4
The Little Book of Irish Wit & Wisdom -
    ISBN 1-85479-827-8
The Little Book of Scottish Wit & Wisdom -
    ISBN 1-85479-826-X

Postage and packing outside the UK:
Europe: add 20% of retail price
Rest of the world: add 30% of retail price

To order any Michael O'Mara Book
please call our credit-card hotline: 020 8324 5652

Michael O'Mara Bookshop
BVCD
32-34 Park Royal Road
London NW10 7LN